IF FOUND PLEASE RETURN TO:

👤 _____

✉ _____

📱 _____

Greater Than a Tourist Book Series
Reviews from Readers

I think the series is wonderful and beneficial for tourists to get information before visiting the city. - Seckin Zumbul, Izmir Turkey

I am a world traveler who has read many trip guides but this one really made a difference for me. I would call it a heartfelt creation of a local guide expert instead of just a guide. -Susy, Isla Holbox, Mexico

New to the area like me, this is a must have! -Joe, Bloomington, USA

This is a good series that gets down to it when looking for things to do at your destination without having to read a novel for just a few ideas. -Rachel, Monterey, USA

Good information to have to plan my trip to this destination. -Pennie Farrell, Mexico

Great ideas for a port day. -Mary Martin USA

Aptly titled, you won't just be a tourist after reading this book. You'll be greater than a tourist! -Alan Warner, Grand Rapids, USA

Even though I only have three days to spend in San Miguel in an upcoming visit, I will use the author's suggestions to guide some of my time there. An easy read - with chapters named to guide me in directions I want to go. -Robert Catapano, USA

Great insights from a local perspective! Useful information and a very good value! -Sarah, USA

This series provides an in-depth experience through the eyes of a local. Reading these series will help you to travel the city in with confidence and it'll make your journey a unique one. -Andrew Teoh, Ipoh, Malaysia

GREATER THAN A TOURIST – SANTIAGO CHILE

50 Travel Tips from a Local

Sara Valcourt

Greater Than a Tourist
Visit our website at www.GreaterThanaTourist.com

Lock Haven, PA
ISBN: 9781717797100

>TOURIST

50 TRAVEL TIPS FROM A LOCAL

BOOK DESCRIPTION

Are you excited about planning your next trip?

Do you want to try something new?

Would you like some guidance from a local?

If you answered yes to any of these questions, then this Greater Than a Tourist book is for you.

Greater Than a Tourist Santiago, Chile by Sara Valcourt offers the inside scoop on Santiago Chile. Most travel books tell you how to travel like a tourist. Although there is nothing wrong with that, as part of the Greater Than a Tourist series, this book will give you travel tips from someone who has lived at your next travel destination.

In these pages, you will discover advice that will help you throughout your stay. This book will not tell you exact addresses or store hours but instead will give you excitement and knowledge from a local that you may not find in other smaller print travel books.

Travel like a local. Slow down, stay in one place, and get to know the people and the culture. By the time you finish this book, you will be eager and prepared to travel to your next destination.

TABLE OF CONTENTS

DEDICATION

This book is dedicated to Abner. Thank you for sticking by me. I can't wait for our next Adventure!.

ABOUT THE AUTHOR

Sara is a former ESL teacher who lived in Chile for 4 years. She is an avid traveler who enjoys biking, yoga, hiking and basically anything outdoors. After living in a small beach city in northern Chile, she decided to change it up and move to the capital, Santiago. Santiago was a great place to teach English. Most companies are requiring English these days and it was an opportunity to meet tons of new and interesting people. She stayed in Santiago for one year before returning back to the United States with her husband.

HOW TO USE THIS BOOK

The Greater Than a Tourist book series was written by someone who has lived in an area for over three months. The goal of this book is to help travelers either dream or experience different locations by providing opinions from a local. The author has made suggestions based on their own experiences. Please do your own research before traveling to the area in case the suggested places are unavailable.

FROM THE PUBLISHER

Traveling can be one of the most important parts of a person's life. The anticipation and memories that you have are some of the best. As a publisher of the Greater Than a Tourist book series, as well as the popular 50 Things to Know book series, we strive to help you learn about new places, spark your imagination, and inspire you. Wherever you are and whatever you do I wish you safe, fun, and inspiring travel.

Lisa Rusczyk Ed. D.
CZYK Publishing

OUR STORY

Traveling is a passion of the "Greater than a Tourist" series creator. Lisa studied abroad in college, and for their honeymoon Lisa and her husband toured Europe. During her travels to Malta, an older man tried to give her some advice based on his own experience living on the island since he was a young boy. She was not sure if she should talk to the stranger but was interested in his advice. When traveling to some places she was wary to talk to locals because she was afraid that they weren't being genuine. Through her travels, Lisa learned how much locals had to share with tourists. Lisa created the "Greater Than a Tourist" book series to help connect people with locals. A topic that locals are very passionate about sharing.

WELCOME TO
> TOURIST

"When all's said and done, all roads lead to the same end. So it's not so much which road you take, as how you take it."

— Charles de Lint

1. GETTING TO/FROM THE AIRPORT

There are a lot of options for people to get to and from the airport in Santiago. If you're on a budget there are two buses you can take Centro Puerto and Turbus. The Centro Puerto will take you as far as Los Heroes metro station and Turbus will take you to Terminal Alameda, which are both in the downtown area. You can also take a shared transfer. This is more expensive but it takes you directly to your accommodation. The most comfortable and convenient but also the most expensive is to take a private taxi or private transfer from the airport. Uber is always an option but it is illegal in Chile and the police are extremely strict about it. They are constantly at the airport looking for Uber drivers, so I think it's better to just to avoid it especially if you're Spanish isn't the best.

2. WHEN TO VISIT

Since Chile is such a long country the climate from the North to South is extremely different. Santiago has a pretty mild winter but the summers can get pretty hot. I think from March to early May is the best time to come to visit Santiago, depending on what you're trying to see in Chile. From March-May there is still a lot of sun and nice weather but it is not even close to as hot as it is in the summer (December-February). A lot of people just do a stop over in Santiago to go the South or Patagonia, which is best to visit in the summer because the weather can be so unpredictable, but if you're planning to take your trip up north, I would definitely recommend from March to May so you can avoid the sun a bit.

3. WEATHER

Santiago is in the center of Chile so you'll get colder weather than the North in winter but much more comfortable than the South. Since Chile is in the Southern Hemisphere the seasons are opposite so you will get summer in December, January, February and winter in June, July, August. Summers in Santiago can get pretty intense. The sun is super strong and you can get some extremely hot days. Chile has the

Atacama Desert, the driest desert in the world, so there is not much humidity. March to May is a comfortable time in Santiago because you still have the sun but it's much less intense than in the summertime. If you're used to winters in a colder country, you will probably be pretty comfortable in Santiago during winter. The morning will normally be pretty cold between mid 30s-40s F (5-10 C) but if the sun comes out it could be in the 60s F (20s C) during the day. You will see more rain in the wintertime but it's not every day. During springtime (September-November) you will get pretty up and down weather like most other countries during spring.

4. CHILEAN SUN

Chile probably has the strongest sun I have felt out of any country I have ever traveled too. If you have light, sensitive skin in, you need to be extremely careful. If you're going to be in the sun wear sunscreen and try to cover up as much as possible because you will get burnt. Even though Santiago is not technically part of the Desert climate, you're still going to get that type of sun in the summer.

5. SUNDAYS

Since Santiago is the capital city of Chile, it can get pretty crowded. Sundays are great because many things are closed but you can roam around the city at a much more relaxing pace than you could do during a weekday. If you just want to walk around the city and explore what it looks like, Sunday would be a nice option. One place that is nice to go is Calle Bandera or Bandera Street. This is Pedestrian Street that has been painted with different colors and designs and has several unique looking structures. It is downtown Santiago so on the weekdays it's pretty crowded but on Sunday you can really enjoy the scenery.

6. PROVIDENCIA, LAS CONDES

Two of the nicest parts of Santiago are Providencia and Las Condes. They are cleaner, better connected and have more to do. Providencia is probably the main area where most people stay because they have a wide variety of hostels but there are a lot of nice hotels in Las Condes. Las Condes is beautiful, well maintained area. Providencia and Las Condes are both reachable on metro line 1(the red line).

7. WHERE TO STAY

Santiago has good options for all types of travelers. If you're a backpacker there are several options to choose from for a decent hostel and if you sleep in a dorm it shouldn't be pretty affordable. For people wanting to spend a little more money or that want more privacy, Airbnb is also a great option. You could rent a room for a more budget friendly price or if you want to splurge a bit, you can rent a whole apartment. Most of the people who rent spaces consistently on Airbnb speak English so you should be able to work things out relatively easily. Finally, you can always stay in a hotel. This is definitely the most expensive option but also the most luxurious. They have a lot of the popular hotels like the Ritz Carlton, Hyatt and Marriot but also some strictly Chilean hotels like Hotel Singular. If you're looking to save money you can always try couch surfing. Over half of the Chilean population Chile lives just in Santiago so there should be at least one person willing to host you.

8. PUBLIC TRANSPORT

Santiago has a pretty cheap and reliable public transportation system compared to other places. The metro is pretty consistent and fast on the weekdays but still runs every 10-15 minutes on the weekends. The prices vary depending on the time of day. It's the most expensive during peak hours (7:00 am- 9:00 am & 6:00 pm- 8:00 pm). The buses are the same prices but you can also combine trips. So if you need to take the metro and then transfer to a bus it won't cost you extra. If you're on a budget, it's a great option and most routes are on Google maps so you can always double check that you're going the right way.

9. "CHILENO"

One of the first things you will learn about Chile is that speak differently than other Spanish speaking countries. They use a lot of slang (or chilenismos), change the pronunciation of words, speak very fast and change the pronunciation of some words. For example, instead of saying "como estas" (how are you) they'll say "como estai". They tend to drop the 's' off of a lot of words. Even native Spanish speakers from other countries have told me they had problems understanding the Chileans when they first arrived, so even if you're comfortable with your Spanish, give yourself time to adjust in Chile.

10. CHILENISMOS

One thing people notice in Chile, Spanish speaking or not, is that they don't understand a lot of the words people are using or why they are using them in a specific context. That is because there is a lot of slang or "chilenismos" in Chileno. It is not that hard to adjust to but you will probably need some time to get used to it. Some common words are: Cachay, which is similar to you know? (entiendes); fome, which means boring (aburrido); Cuatico, which means something is complicated or dangerous (complicado/peligroso); Seco, which is like something or someone is really good or an expert. The original meaning of seco is dry so you'll need to pay attention to the context; Caleta, which means it's a lot or too much (mucho); Huea (pronounced we-a), this is one of the most common things you'll hear in Chile and can be used to substitute a word for an object ex: esta rica la huea (this is really good). It can also be used to talk about something you really like or when you don't agree with someone. Hueon (pronounced way-on), normally used when talking to a friend, can be offensive if you call someone you don't know well this. Al tiro, means something will happen immediately (immediatamente.) These are just a few but be prepared to learn a lot of new words and phrases!

11. SPEAKING ENGLISH

Like I said before, Chilean Spanish can be difficult to understand at first no matter what your level is. If you really have no idea what's going on, you can always try to speak English. You might not always find someone who speaks well but a lot of Chileans don't mind practicing so it doesn't hurt to try. Since Santiago is the capital city and there are a lot of international companies, you should be able to find a good amount of people who speak decently or at least understand. Obviously if you're in a touristy area, you won't have many problems.

12. GET TO KNOW PEOPLE

Chile was a closed off country for a long time and it wasn't until recently that tourism became a real thing in Santiago. Some Chileans still have never met a foreigner outside of Latin America and are always very interested when they meet someone from a different continent. A lot of people's only impression is from what they see on TV so be prepared for some interesting questions and people who want to practice their English. They truly are just curious and want to learn about something different.

13. LA VEGA

A good way to save money on your produce is to go to "La Vega". This is a huge market in downtown Santiago that sells everything. I don't eat meat so I don't know if it's cheaper there, but there definitely is a huge difference in price and quality of the fruits and vegetables at the market. They buy in bulk at the market so you can get some really great deals and the food is definitely fresher. The nice thing about this market is that they have signs with the prices per kilo for each item so there is a less of a chance that they'll try to cheat you because you're a foreigner. I would recommend trying to go in the morning on the weekday so you can take your time looking for your food and not worry about crowds from the weekend.

14. ASADOS

Asados, or barbeques, are one of the most, if not the most popular way for Chileans to celebrate almost anything. Birthday parties, soccer matches, or just the weekend. Really an asado is an event of itself. Normally you start with a chorizo or choripan, which is just sausage in bun with some type of sauce on top. After that Normally there will be chicken, ribs, pork and probably some steak. And of course there is always beer, wine and pisco. So don't fill up too much at the beginning because you'll be eating all night!

15. FOOD

Chile is a meat eating country. Meat is eaten everyday, sometimes multiple times a day. The Asados are always an option when you over to someone's house. Some other typical dishes are: salchipapas, which is a dish with french fries at the bottom and is usually topped with a variety of meats normally hot dogs, sausages and some type of beef and an egg done over easy; porotos con rienda , a bean soup/stew with pasta; Ensalada a la chilena ,a salad made with raw onions and tomatoes ; Pastel de choclo , kind of like a shepard's pie but made with pureed corn and normally has grown beef, olives and a hard boiled egg in it; Cazuela, which is a soup that contains either a piece of chicken or beef, a small chopped piece of corn, a piece of potato , sometimes a piece of squash and green beans. These are all hardy dishes that should leave you full until dinner.

16. RESTAURANTS

Being a big city, Santiago is full of different types of restaurants. There is a good variety of international food including: Arabic, sushi, Indian, Italian, American, Chinese, Peruvian, Argentinian and Columbian and more. If you're looking for restaurants with more traditional Chilean dishes some well known places are: Los Buenos Muchachos, The Mercado Central which is close to La Vega, El Caramaño and Don Peyo. Those are just some options but you will see tons of local places walking around the downtown area.

17. STREET FOOD

The two most popular street food options you will find in Santiago are sopaipillas and empanadas. Sopaipillas are basically just fried dough made into circles which you can put toppings on including

mustard, mayo or some type of pebre (a spicy sauce).
They are super cheap, delicious and filling.

Empanadas are also a common option. On the street
they are normally sold with cheese but you can find
other options in the empanada shops. In these places
you can find empanadas filled with chicken, seafood
and beef (which is called pino). Although not as
common to find in Santiago on the street, a completo
is always a popular option for someone on the go.
This is hotdog normally topped with mayo, avocado,
tomato and sauerkraut. In the mornings, there are
many people selling fruit or yogurt in a cup, as well
as coffee and sandwiches. There are also little kiosks
that are up all day where you can buy snacks like
chips, cookies, juices and nuts.

18. BREAD

One of the top things Chileans will tell you to try
is their bread. Chileans always have freshly baked
bread in their homes and eat it everyday. You can
find bread in any major supermarket chain or in the
small "almacenes" or corner stores they have. There
are also some "panaderias" or bakeries that only sell
baked goods. It really depends on where you go.
Some places just sell the generic typical types, and

others sell some really good quality stuff. My favorite is "amasado" which is denser bread that they knead. It has a nice texture and taste. Also, another good quality bread is one made with "masa madre". This is vegan and normally a much healthier option because it is made with wheat and seeds.

19. SUPERMARKETS

The four big supermarket chains in Santiago are Lider (which is owned by walmart), Tottus, Jumbo and Santa Isabel. In downtown Santiago they mostly have express versions of the stores so sometimes they have less selections but normally have all the essentials. If you're looking for more specialty items, Jumbo is the place to go. The Jumbo in Costanera center is definitely the best in the city. It has the most diverse selection. You can find all types of products there but you might be paying a lot more than you would at home. But sometimes it's worth it.

20. VEGETARIAN OPTIONS

Chile is a huge meat eating country but there are definitely more people changing to a vegetarian/vegan diet. On the lunch menus, there are more vegetarian options than before. Vegan is definitely more difficult to find but there are more vegan/vegetarian restaurants popping up. One option is El Huerto, which is vegetarian with vegan options and has fresh natural ingredients. Many of the sushi places will let you customize your sushi and there are more Indian restaurants popping out that lean naturally more vegetarian.

21. BOTTLED VS. TAP WATER

Drinking tap water in Santiago is safe but many people don't like to do it because they don't like the taste. I personally drank mostly tap water and never had any problems. I don't believe in paying for water so if the water is safe, I will drink it. It's really up to your personal preference but you shouldn't get sick from it. They also sell brita filters if you don't want to use plastic bottles but still are a little nervous about drinking from the tap.

22. GOING OUT

Santiago is a very social place and people go out for drinks and food everyday of the week. If you're looking to go out for a drink or some food some of the most popular areas are Avenida Brasil, Lastarria and Bellavista. There are also some popular places to

go to close to Costanera Center/Tobalaba metro
station. If you're looking for dancing, Santiago is full
of nightclubs or discotheques for all types of people.
Blondie is a famous club in the city that is known for
being very free and accepting of all lifestyles.

23. WINE/WINERIES

Chile is one of the most well known wine
countries is the world. They are most famous for their
red wine. It is easy to find nice wine for decent prices
in all super markets are liquor stores in Santiago. But
if you're looking to learn more about the production
process, luckily there are several wineries close to
Santiago. Cousiño Macul is the closest to the city
being only 14 km outside the city. Other options that
are all about 40 km outside the city are Unduragga,
Santa Rita and Concho y Toro. They all offer tours
but make sure to call ahead to make sure you don't
need a reservation.

24. PISCO

Besides wine, Chileans love to drink Pisco. Two of
the most popular drinks are a "Piscola" which you
probably guessed is pisco mixed with coca-cola and a

"Pisco Sour." Like wine, you can get pisco very cheap at almost any grocery store or botilleria (liquor store). If you have a more sophisticated palate you might want to try some pisco from the Elqui Valley (Valle de Elqui). This is where most of the grapes are grown and they tend to make a higher quality product.

25. PATRONATO

Close to "La Vega" There is the metro station called Patronato. This area is a great place to go if you're looking to find some cheap items like clothes, bags, shoes, jewelry and watches. If you have forgotten something but don't want pay too much this could be a great place to check out. You'll get decent clothes that you could probably just leave at a hostel or give to a fellow traveler after you're done with your trip.

26. HOW TO SAVE MONEY

A lot of times when people think of South America they think it's going to be cheap. Unfortunately that's not the case in Chile and several other countries in South America. If you plan on going to any part of Chile, be prepared to spend about the same amount of money you would pay in the US or Europe. Santiago is no exception. A Dorm room in a hostel can be decently priced in Santiago and like I said earlier, you can get some good savings at "La Vega". If you're trying to travel on a budget but aren't much of a cook, definitely go for the menu options most restaurants have during lunchtime. Obviously if you are in the more touristy areas you'll spend more but if you go to a more local place, you'll be able to spend about half the price for a decent amount of food. Most menus include a drink, appetizer (like a salad or soup), a main course and a dessert. I wouldn't recommend buying a lot of clothes or cosmetics while you're there unless you have no other option. Things like toothpaste, floss, deodorant and shampoos; pads/tampons can be double the price for lower quality and quantity. The clothes situation is the same. They sell products that you can get in The US or Europe for sometimes triple the price and the quality is much worse. My advice is to come prepared and save your money to spend on the more fun parts of your trip.

27. CURRENCY

The Chilean Peso is used in Chile. Bills come in denominations of thousands (1000, 2000, 5000, 10000, 20000). In coins there are 1, 5, 10, 50, 100, 500 pieces. The 1 and 5 peso coins are being phased out though. 1.000 clp is about a $1.50 usd. The convenient thing about Chilean money is that is color-coded. The green bill is 1.000, purple is 2.000, pink is 5.000, blue is 10.000 and orange is 20.000. It is always good to have cash in small bills and in Chile and coins are actually extremely useful especially if you're paying in the small corner markets for just a few items. Some places will not have change for even a 20.

28. CASH VS. CREDIT

If you're bank is not very flexible about ATM charges, I would definitely bring cash. The foreign card charges are ridiculously high. The Banco de Chile surcharges are the most expensive. It is very easy to find a legitimate place to exchange your money in Santiago so I would just recommend bringing cash or just using your card. AFEX is a common currency exchange that you can find in the Santiago Airport and in downtown Santiago. If you're having problems finding one just ask where a "casa de cambio" is. If you have a credit card (Visa or MasterCard) that doesn't have international fees you should be able to use it at most places in Santiago. Other parts of Chile aren't so card friendly.

29. WIFI

Santiago is a very connected city. People are always on their phones. For that reason, you shouldn't have that hard of a time trying to find wifi. There are a lot of chains in Chile like Starbucks that always have wifi as well as most restaurants will give the wifi password if you ask. The only thing is that you'll have to buy something to use it.

30. PREPAID MOBILE SIM CARDS

Chile has some pretty decent prepaid phone plans. If you're worried about getting lost or just like to be connected and your phone is unlocked, you can always get a prepaid phone card. Some of the most popular companies are Claro, Entel and Wom. In downtown Santiago they have all the phone companies offices and you can just ask for a sim card.

31. STAYING SAFE

Since there are more people coming to the capital, the crime rate has gone up like most major cities. I personally never had any problems, but I have met a lot of people who have been robbed or assaulted. Just be careful. If you act like you know where you're going and what you're doing, it'll make a huge difference. Sometimes it is a situation of being in the wrong place at the wrong time, but I really do believe if you are just aware of your surroundings you should be fine. Pickpocketing is big in Santiago, Chile and in South America in general so just make sure you don't have your phone or wallet just hanging out where anyone can just grab it. The metro and common tourist attractions like Cerro San Cristobal are common places where tourists and Chileans have had their things stolen. Also, Starbucks is a popular place for thieves because people tend to get distracted by work or conversation and tend to bring expensive items like their computers. So again just keep your eyes peeled and be aware of what's going on around you and you should be fine.

32. UBER

Like I said before, Uber is illegal in Chile. There are a lot issues between the taxi and Uber drivers because Ubers are becoming much more popular than taxis. I used it a lot in Santiago and never had any real issues anywhere else besides the airport. I wouldn´t be scared to use it but just be aware of the situation. Santiago definitely has the strictest rules regarding Uber compared to the rest of the country.

33. TIPPING

The only places where Chileans tip are in restaurants and hotels. The nice thing about the restaurants is that they include it in the bill so you don't have to do any extra math. It is not necessary to give a tip and they will always ask you if you want to include it. It's only 10% so I would give it anyways.

34. BEACHES

Santiago can get pretty overwhelming at times since it's a big city but luckily Santiago is less than 2 hours away from Valparaiso and Viña del Mar. They are probably the most popular beach areas in Chile and are very well maintained. Buses run from

Pajaritos station (which is on the metro line 1) almost all day so you won't have any problems getting there or getting back. Be prepared if you're planning to go in the summer because it will be packed!

35. PARKS

There are a lot of nice parks in Santiago to go to and relax in. The nicest ones in my opinion are Parque O´higgins, Forestal, Araucano and Bicentenario. O´higgins is located in downtown Santiago. It is a big park where they hold a lot of special events like Lollapalooza, Independence Day celebrations, host special guests like the pope etc. The amusement park Fantasilandia is also connected to Parque O'higgins. Parque Forestal is in Providencia and runs parallel to the Mapocho River. There are a lot of trees and it's just a nice place to go and sit and relax. They also hold events like jazz festivals, yoga classes and have activities for kids on the weekends. Parque Araucano is probably my favorite on this list. If you're an active person, this is the park for you. There are soccer, tennis and basketball courts, outdoor exercise equipment and a calisthenics bar area. There are playgrounds for the kids and in the middle of the park they have a restaurant area and an inside area with a rock climbing gym. Parque Bicentenario is probably the most aesthetically pleasing of the parks. It is in Vitacura and has beautiful yellow flowers surrounding the area. You have a great view of the mountains on one side and then there is a nice view of the city on the other. This is probably the best park in Santiago to go to and just relax.

36. VISIT LASTARRIA

One of my personal favorite places to go to in Santiago is Lastarria. It has a completely different vibe from the rest of Santiago. There are a lot of restaurants, good places to get a drink, and people selling handmade jewelry, teas, sauces, cosmetic products and art. There is an old movie theater called "El Biografo" which plays maybe 1 or 2 different movies at a time, normally in English, and it's a bit cheaper than the normal theaters. Merced, the street perpendicular to Lastarria, also has some fun shops, vegan/organic stores and restaurants you can check out.

37. COSTANERA CENTER

Another popular attraction in Santiago is Costanera Center. This is the biggest mall in Chile and the tallest building in South America. Costanera is six floors high and is full of all the most popular international stores including H&M, Forever 21, Top Shop etc. It is also has a jumbo which definitely has the best variety and options for your food shopping. If you don't want to shop, you can go to the top floor and see a beautiful view of Santiago. Costanera is located in Las Condes close to the Tobalaba metro station. This is a top spot in Santiago for Tourists and locals.

38. HIKING

Santiago is surrounded by the Andes Mountains so there are a lot of options for hiking. One popular option that you can get to by public bus is Parque Aguas de Ramon. There are 3 trails varying in time and difficulty. If you want to do the longest one (16.5 km) you need to get there early, probably around 8:00 am because it takes about 7 hours without breaks and they close the park at 6:00pm. Another option is to head a little farther to head over to Cajon del Maipo. This is a big park with multiple treks and outdoor natural baths. It is possible to take a bus to San Jose de Maipo and get a tour from there. You can take a bus from the metro stations Bellavista de la Florida (Line 5), Las Mercedes (Line 4) or

Plaza de Puente Alto (Line 4). From here you can take a bus or colectivo (cheaper version of a taxi where they take multiple going to different locations on a specific route.) There are only specific areas you can get to without a car or tour so do your research before.

39. MUSEUMS

Chile has an interesting history politically and culturally so stopping into a museum or two when in Santiago should be on your to do list if you have the time. Parque Quinta Normal has most of the popular museums in the city. It's very easy to get to you just need to get off the Parque Quinta Normal metro station on line 5. One of my favorites is the Museum of Memory and Human Rights (Museo de la Memoria y los Derechos Humanos). It goes into a detailed history of the Dictatorship led by Augusto Pinochet. This is a museum that you could go 2, 3, 4 times and still learn something new. Most museums are free which is great. Two popular museums that you do need to pay for are Museo Chileno de Arte Precolombino and La Chascona, which is one of Pablo Neruda's houses. If you have time, definitely try and see it.

40. YOGA, MEDITATION, HOLISTIC THERAPIES

The yoga and holistic movement has definitely hit Santiago. There are so many different yoga studios, places for sound therapy, reiki and for meditation. There are surely places that are similar to the prices in the US but there are also a lot cheaper options and free events going on in the city. Yuukti yoga is a good option if you want to find classses for cheap. Also in the summer, a lot of studios have deals. If you're going to be in Santiago for a while, definitely do some research and see what types of events and deals you can find. Classes are done in Spanish but if you get confused, you can always just look around the class to see what the other students are doing.

41. CERRO SAN CRISTOBAL

Cerro San Cristobal is a big park and has several options to get to the top. It is free to enter if you walk up the hill or bike. There are some trekking trails that you can take that should take no more than a couple of hours based on your fitness level. Another popular option is to take the teleferico (cable cars) to the top. This is a nice option because you'll get to see most of the city. It's not that expensive and definitely worth the ride in my opinion. The only thing to consider is that this is a huge tourist spot for Chileans and foreigners so the weekends/holidays can get pretty crazy. People also talk about there being pickpockets so again just use common sense and keep an eye on your belongings. I have never personally felt unsafe there.

42. SANTA LUCIA

Santa Lucia is a small park with statues, fountains and formed around an old castle. It is an easy 10-15 min walk to get to the top and you can get some nice views of the city. It's free and right in the center of Santiago by the Santa Lucia or Universidad Catolica metro stations. Try to go on a weekday because you can really take your time and enjoy your views at the top without having to deal with the crowds.

43. CONCERTS-LIVE MUSIC

There are a lot of musicians in Santiago and a lot of people who love live music. Most bars on the weekend with have a local band playing. They also have a lot of events in the park from jazz festivals to local rock bands. If you're not so into the local music don't worry. Movistar Arena hosts most famous artists from Guns n Roses to Arcade Fire to Katy Perry. They also host Lollapalooza every year in Parque O'higgins.

44. GETTING IN A WORKOUT

There are a lot of active people in Santiago, like in most cities, so if you're itching to get in a workout while traveling, you shouldn't have any problems. There are tons of options for gyms. Pacific is a 24-hour gym that has locations all over the city with day passes. If you're like me and prefer to be outside, you can run or bike along ciclovia mapocho, workout out on the outside exercise equipment, go for a hike along some of the trails in or just outside the city, join in on a soccer, basketball or tennis match, or go to a yoga class.

45. BOOK STORES

Downtown Santiago is full of bookstores and people selling books on the street. If you're looking to practice your Spanish reading skills you should have no problems trying to find something that interests you. The bookstores can get a bit pricey so if you're able to find a book vendor on the street with a good selection definitely check them out first. Also, I have heard that books written in English tend to be cheaper than the ones written in Spanish, so if you're just looking for a book just to relax or pass time with, you could find some good deals!

46. SOUVENIRS

If you're looking for souvenirs, you shouldn't have to look too far in Santiago. The Santa Lucia Market (right across from the hill) has tons of options from trinkets to clothing and jewelry. If you're looking for a more boutique feel, you can head over to Patio Bellavista or Lastarria. There you will find artisan jewelry and some handmade clothes. At the top of Cerro San Cristobal they have some shops that sell the typical trinkets if you just want a little something to remember your trip by.

47. SEPTEMBER 18TH

The biggest holiday by far in Chile is September 18th or dieciocho in spanish. This is the Chilean Independence Day. Once September hits you will see stores filled with decorations for the holiday. Normally schools will let out for at least 2-3 days or sometimes even a week depending on what day it lands on. There are parades and celebrations and people do some serious partying. To celebrate the 18th, Chileans have several barbeques, eat lots of traditional foods, drink a lot of wine, pisco and terremotos (white wine with pineapple sherbet), and chicha(fermented alcohol),spend time with family and friends and dance Cueca. This is definitely a crazy but fun time to be in any part of Chile.

48. CUECA

If you spend some time in Chile, you'll end up seeing someone dancing Cueca. Cueca is the national dance of Chile, which you will see in all regions of the country. Cueca is traditionally done in pairs with a man and women who are dressed in traditional ranch clothing. When the music starts the pair starts to walk and are "getting to know each other" like a first date. The pair walks with their arms linked and after they separate and face each other but from a modest distance. At this point the pair starts to clap to the rhythm of the music. When the singer starts to sing, the pair will take a handkerchief and swing it over their heads moving in a circular motion. The idea of the dance is that the man is trying to win the heart of the women. Cueca is done during parades in the street but you can also see it in several places in Santiago like La Casa de la Cueca, Club Matadero, Bar Victoria and Fonda Permanente.

49. TEACHING ENGLISH

Like most countries, learning English has become a very important part of Chilean culture. There are tons of international companies and tourism is increasing meaning that Chileans need to start learning English. If you plan on being in Santiago long term or at least for a few months, becoming an English teacher could be a great option for you to make some extra money for your travels. Most places want someone with experience or at least a TEFL certificate, but there are always companies that need Native/Advanced English speakers. To work at an academy you will normally need to have at least a temporary visa, so that is something to consider. Another great option for people with experience is to teach private English classes or "clases particulares" in spanish. There are a lot of people who don't want to or can't because of their work schedule go to an academy hence they often try to find private English teachers. This is nice because they will pay you in cash (or a bank transfer if you have a chilean account) and you can make your own schedule.

50. WHATSAPP

Whatsapp is basically life in Chile and Santiago. Most people communicate through whatsapp and things can get inconvenient if you don't have the app. If you don't plan on buying a sim card when you're in the city, download the app before you get to Santiago so you can use your home number to set up your account. You can use it over wifi, so if you meet some new friends in the city, you can stay in touch with them!

BONUS BOOK

50 THINGS TO KNOW ABOUT PACKING LIGHT FOR TRAVEL

PACK THE RIGHT WAY EVERY TIME

AUTHOR: MANIDIPA BHATTACHARYYA

Edited by Melanie Howthorne

ABOUT THE AUTHOR

Manidipa Bhattacharyya is a creative writer and editor, with an
education in English literature and Linguistics. After working in the IT
industry for seven long years she decided to call it quits and follow her
heart instead. Manidipa has been ghost writing, editing, proof reading
and doing secondary research services for many story tellers and article
writers for about three years. She stays in Kolkata, India with her
husband and a busy two year old. In her own time Manidipa enjoys
travelling, photography and writing flash fiction.

Manidipa believes in travelling light and never carries anything that she
couldn't haul herself on a trip. However, travelling with her child
changed the scenario. She seemed to carry the entire world with her for
the baby on the first two trips. But good sense prevailed and she is
again working her way to becoming a light traveler, this time with a
kid.

INTRODUCTION

He who would travel happily
must travel light.

-Antoine de Saint-Exupéry

Travel takes you to different places from seas and mountains to deserts and much more. In your travels you get to interact with different people and their cultures. You will, however, enjoy the sights and interact positively with these new people even more, if you are travelling light.

When you travel light your mind can be free from worry about your belongings. You do not have to spend precious vacation time waiting for your luggage to arrive after a long flight. There is be no chance of your bags going missing and the best part is that you need not pay a fee for checked baggage.

People who have mastered this art of packing light will root for you to take only one carry-on, wherever you go. However, many people can find it really hard to pack light. More so if you are travelling with children. Differentiating between "must have" and "just in case" items is the starting point. There will be ample shopping avenues at your destination which are just waiting to be explored.

47

This book will show you 'packing' in a new 'light' –
pun intended – and help you to embrace light
packing practices for all of your future travels.

Off to packing!

DEDICATION

I dedicate this book to all the travel buffs that I know,
who have given me great insights into the contents of
their backpacks.

THE RIGHT TRAVEL GEAR

1. CHOOSE YOUR TRAVEL GEAR CAREFULLY

While selecting your travel gear, pick items that are
light weight, durable and most importantly, easy to
carry. There are cases with wheels so you can drag
them along – these are usually on the heavy side
because of the trolley. Alternatively a backpack that
you can carry comfortably on your back, or even a
duffel bag that you can carry easily by hand or sling
across your body are also great options. Whatever
you choose, one thing to keep in mind is that the
luggage itself should not weigh a ton, this will give
you the flexibility to bring along one extra pair of
shoes if you so desire.

2. CARRY THE MINIMUM NUMBER OF BAGS

Selecting light weight luggage is not everything. You need to restrict the number of bags you carry as well. One carry-on size bag is ideal for light travel. Most carriers allow one cabin baggage plus one purse, handbag or camera bag as long as it slides under the seat in front. So technically, you can carry two items of luggage without checking them in.

3. PACK ONE EXTRA BAG

Always pack one extra empty bag along with your essential items. This could be a very light weight duffel bag or even a sturdy tote bag which takes up minimal space. In the event that you end up buying a lot of souvenirs, you already have a handy bag to stuff all that into and do not have to spend time hunting for an appropriate bag.

I'm very strict with my packing and have everything in its right place. I never change a rule. I hardly use anything in the hotel room. I wheel my own wardrobe in and that's it.

Charlie Watts

CLOTHES & ACCESSORIES

4. PLAN AHEAD

Figure out in advance what you plan to do on your trip. That will help you to pick that one dress you need for the occasion. If you are going to attend a wedding then you have to carry formal wear. If not, you can ditch the gown for something lighter that will be comfortable during long walks or on the beach.

5. WEAR THAT JACKET

Remember that wearing items will not add extra luggage for your air travel. So wear that bulky jacket that you plan to carry for your trip. This saves space and can also help keep you warm during the chilly flight.

6. MIX AND MATCH

Carry clothes that can be interchangeably used to reinvent your look. Find one top that goes well with a couple of pairs of pants or skirts. Use tops, shirts and jackets wisely along with other accessories like a scarf or a stole to create a new look.

7. CHOOSE YOUR FABRIC WISELY

Stuffing clothes in cramped bags definitely takes its toll which results in wrinkles. It is best to carry wrinkle free, synthetic clothes or merino tops. This will eliminate the need for that small iron you usually bring along.

8. DITCH CLOTHES PACK UNDERWEAR

Pack more underwear and socks. These are the things that will give you a fresh feel even if you do not get a chance to wear fresh clothes. Moreover these are easy to wash and can be dried inside the hotel room itself.

9. CHOOSE DARK OVER LIGHT

While picking your clothes choose dark coloured ones. They are easy to colour coordinate and can last longer before needing a wash. Accidental food spills and dirt from the road are less visible on darker clothes.

10. WEAR YOUR JEANS

Take only one pair of Jeans with you, which you should wear on the flight. Remember to pick a pair that can be worn for sightseeing trips and is equally eloquent for dinner. You can add variety by adding light weight cargoes and chinos.

11. CARRY SMART ACCESSORIES

The right accessory can give you a fresh look even with the same old dress. An intelligent neck-piece, a couple of bright scarves, stoles or a sarong can be used in a number of ways to add variety to your clothing. These light weight beauties can double up as a nursing cover, a light blanket, beach wear, a modesty cover for visiting places of worship, and also makes for an enthralling game of peek-a-boo.

12. LEARN TO FOLD YOUR GARMENTS

Seasoned travellers all swear by rolling their clothes for compact and wrinkle free packing. Bundle packing, where you roll the clothes around a central object as if tying it up, is also a popular method of compact and wrinkle free packing. Stacking folded clothes one on top of another is a big no-no as it makes creases extreme and they are difficult to get rid of without ironing.

13. WASH YOUR DIRTY LAUNDRY

One of the ways to avoid carrying loads of clothes is to wash the clothes you carry. At some places you might get to use the laundry services or a Laundromat but if you are in a pinch, best solution is to wash them yourself. If that is the plan then carrying quick drying clothes is highly recommended, which most often also happen to be the wrinkle free variety.

14. LEAVE THOSE TOWELS BEHIND

Regular towels take up a lot of space, are heavy and take ages to dry out. If you are staying at hotels they will provide you with towels anyway. If you are travelling to a remote place, where the availability of towels look doubtful, carry a light weight travel towel of viscose material to do the job.

15. USE A COMPRESSION BAG

Compression bags are getting lots of recommendation now days from regular travellers. These are useful for saving space in your luggage when you have to pack bulky dresses. While packing for the return trip, get help from the hotel staff to arrange a vacuum cleaner.

FOOTWEAR

16. PUT ON YOUR HIKING BOOTS

If you have plans to go hiking or trekking during your trip, you will need those bulky hiking boots. The best way to carry them is to wear them on flight to save space and luggage weight. You can remove the boots once inside and be comfortable in your socks.

17. PICKING THE RIGHT SHOES

Shoes are often the bulkiest items, along with being the dainty if you are a female. They need care and take up a lot of space in your luggage. It is advisable therefore to pick shoes very carefully. If you plan to do a lot of walking and site seeing, then wearing a pair of comfortable walking shoes are a must. For more formal occasions you can carry durable, light weight flats which will not take up much space.

18. STUFF SHOES

If you happen to pack a pair of shoes, ensure you utilize their hollow insides. Tuck small items like rolled up socks or belts to save space. They will also be easy to find.

TOILETRIES

19. STASHING TOILETRIES

Carry only absolute necessities. Airline rules dictate
that for one carry-on bag, liquids and gels must be in
3.4 ounce (100ml) bottles or less, and must be packed
in a one quart zip-lock bag. If you are planning to stay
in a hotel, the basic things will be provided for you.
It's best is to buy the rest from the local market at
your destination.

20. TAKE ALONG TAMPONS

Tampons are a hard to find item in a lot of countries.
Figure out how many you need and pack accordingly.
For longer stays you can buy them online and have
them delivered to where you are staying.

21. GET PAMPERED BEFORE YOU TRAVEL

Some avid travellers suggest getting a pedicure and
manicure just the day before travelling. This not only
gives you a well kept look, you also save the trouble
of packing nail polish. Remember, every little bit of
weight reduced adds up.

ELECTRONICS
22. LUGGING ALONG ELECTRONICS

Electronics have a large role to play in our lives today. Most of us cannot imagine our lives away from our phones, laptops or tablets. However while travelling, one must consider the amount of weight these electronics add to our luggage. Thankfully smart phones come along with all the essentials tools like a camera, email access, picture editing tools and more. They are smart to the point of eliminating the need to carry multiple gadgets. Choose a smart phone that suits all your requirements and travel with the world in your palms or pocket.

23. REDUCE THE NUMBER OF CHARGERS

If you do travel with multiple electronic devices, you will have to bear the additional burden of carrying all their chargers too. Check if a single charger can be used for multiple devices. You might also consider investing in a pocket charger. These small devices support multiple devices while keeping you charged on the go.

24. TRAVEL FRIENDLY APPS

Along with smart phones come numerous apps, which are immensely helpful in our travels. You name it and you have an app for it at hand – take pictures, sharing with friends and family, torch to light dark roads, maps, checking flight/train times, find hotels and many other things. Use these smart alternatives to traditional items like books to eliminate weight and save space.

I get ideas about what's essential when packing my suitcase.

-Diane von Furstenberg

TRAVELLING WITH KIDS

25. BRING ALONG THE STROLLER

Kids might enjoy walking for a while but they soon tire out and a stroller is the just the right thing for them to rest in while you continue your tour. Strollers also double duty as a luggage carrier and shopping bag holder. Remember to pick a light weight, easy to handle brand of stroller. Better yet, find out in advance if you can rent a stroller at your destination.

26. BRING ONLY ENOUGH DIAPERS FOR YOUR TRIP

Diapers take up a lot of space and add to the weight of your luggage. Therefore it is advisable to carry just enough diapers to last through the trip and a few for afterwards, till you buy fresh stock at your destination. Unless of course you are travelling to a really remote area, in which case you have no choice but to carry the load. Otherwise diapers are something you will find pretty easily.

27. TAKE ONLY A COUPLE OF TOYS

Children are easily attracted by new things in their environment. While travelling they will find numerous 'new' objects to scrutinize and play with. Packing just one favorite toy is enough, or if there is no favorite toy leave out all of them in favor of stories or imaginary games.

28. CARRY KID FRIENDLY SNACKS

Create a small snack counter in your bag to store away quick bites for those sudden hunger pangs. Depending on the child's age this could include chocolates, raisins, dry fruits, granola bars or biscuits. Also keep a bottle of water handy for your little one.

These things do not add much weight and can be adjusted in a handbag or knapsack.

29. GAMES TO CARRY

Create some travel specific, imaginary games if you have slightly grown up children, like spot the attractions. Keep a coloring book and colors handy for in-flight or hotel time. Apps on your smart phone can keep the children engaged with cartoons and story books. Older children are often entertained by games available on phones or tablets. This cuts the weight of luggage down while keeping the kids entertained.

30. LET THE KIDS CARRY THEIR LOAD

A good thing is to start early sharing of responsibilities. Let your child pick a bag of his or her choice and pack it themselves. Keep tabs on what they are stuffing in their bags by asking if they will be using that item on the trip. It could start out being just an entertainment bag initially but with growing years they will learn to sort the useful from the superfluous. Children as little as four can maneuver a small trolley suitcase like a pro- their experience in pull along toys credit. If you are worried that you may be pulling it for them, you may want to start with a backpack.

31. DECIDE ON LOCATION FOR CHILDREN TO SLEEP

While on a trip you might not always get a crib at your destination, and carrying one will make life all the more difficult. Instead call ahead to see if there are any cribs or roll out beds for children. You may even put blankets on the floor. Weave them a story about camping and they will gladly sleep without any trouble.

32. GET BABY PRODUCTS DELIVERED AT YOUR DESTINATION

If you are absolutely paranoid about not getting your favourite variety of diaper or brand of baby food, check out online stores like amazon.com for services in your destination city. You can buy things online ahead of your travel and get them delivered to your hotel upon arrival.

33. FEEDING NEEDS OF YOUR INFANTS

If you are travelling with a breastfed infant, you save the trouble of carrying bottles and bottle sanitization kits. For special food, or medications, you may need to call ahead to make sure you have a refrigerator where you are staying.

34. FEEDING NEEDS OF YOUR TODDLER

With the progression from infancy to toddler, their dietary requirements too evolve. You will have to pack some snacks for travelling time. Fresh fruits and vegetables can be purchased at your destination. Most of the cities you travel to in whichever part of the world, will have baby food products and formulas, available at the local drug-store or the supermarket.

35. PICKING CLOTHES FOR YOUR BABY

Contrary to popular belief, babies can do without many changes of clothes. At the most pack 2 outfits per day. Pack mix and match type clothes for your little one as well. Pick things which are comfortable to wear and quick to dry.

36. SELECTING SHOES FOR YOUR BABY

Like outfits, kids can make do with two pairs of comfortable shoes. If you can get some water resistant shoes it will be best. To expedite drying wet shoes, you can stuff newspaper in them then wrap them with newspaper and leave them to dry overnight.

37. KEEP ONE CHANGE OF CLOTHES HANDY

Travelling with kids can be tricky. Keep a change of clothes for the kids and mum handy in your purse or tote bag. This takes a bit of space in your hand luggage but comes extremely handy in case there are any accidents or spills.

38. LEAVE BEHIND BABY ACCESSORIES

Baby accessories like their bed, bath tub, car seat, crib etc. should be left at home. Many hotels provide a crib on request, while car seats can be borrowed from friends or rented. Babies can be given a bath in the hotel sink or even in the adult bath tub with a little bit of water. If you bring a few bath toys, they can be used in the bath, pool, and out of water. They can also be sanitized easily in the sink.

39. CARRY A SMALL LOAD OF PLASTIC BAGS

With children around there are chances of a number of soiled clothes and diapers. These plastic bags help to sort the dirt from the clean inside your big bag.

These are very light weight and come in handy to other carry stuff as well at times.

PACK WITH A PURPOSE

40. PACKING FOR BUSINESS TRIPS

One neutral-colored suit should suffice. It can be paired with different shirts, ties and accessories for different occasions. One pair of black suit pants could be worn with a matching jacket for the office or with a snazzy top for dinner.

41. PACKING FOR A CRUISE

Most cruises have formal dinners, and that formal dress usually takes up a lot of space. However you might find a tuxedo to rent. For women, a short black dress with multiple accessory options will do the trick.

42. PACKING FOR A LONG TRIP OVER DIFFERENT CLIMATES

The secret packing mantra for travel over multiple climates is layering. Layering traps air around your body creating insulation against the cold. The same light t-shirt that is comfortable in a warmer climate can be the innermost layer in a colder climate.

REDUCE SOME MORE WEIGHT

43. LEAVE PRECIOUS THINGS AT HOME

Things that you would hate to lose or get damaged leave them at home. Precious jewelry, expensive gadgets or dresses, could be anything. You will not require these on your trip. Leave them at home and spare the load on your mind.

44. SEND SOUVENIRS BY MAIL

If you have spent all your money on purchasing souvenirs, carrying them back in the same bag that you brought along would be difficult. Either pack everything in another bag and check it in the airport or get everything shipped to your home. Use an international carrier for a secure transit, but this could be more expensive than the checking fees at the airport.

45. AVOID CARRYING BOOKS

Books equal to weight. There are many reading apps which you can download on your smart phone or tab.

Plus there are gadgets like Kindle and Nook that are thinner and lighter alternatives to your regular book.

CHECK, GET, SET, CHECK AGAIN

46. STRATEGIZE BEFORE PACKING

Create a travel list and prepare all that you think you need to carry along. Keep everything on your bed or floor before packing and then think through once again – do I really need that? Any item that meets this question can be avoided. Remove whatever you don't really need and pack the rest.

47. TEST YOUR LUGGAGE

Once you have fully packed for the trip take a test trip with your luggage. Take your bags and go to town for window shopping for an hour. If you enjoy your hour long trip it is good to go, if not, go home and reduce the load some more. Repeat this test till you hit the right weight.

48. ADD A ROLL OF DUCT TAPE

You might wonder why, when this book has been talking about reducing stuff, we're suddenly asking you to pack something totally unusual. This is because when you have limited supplies, duct tape is immensely helpful for small repairs – a broken bag, leaking zip-lock bag, broken sunglasses, you name it and duct tape can fix it, temporarily.

49. LIST OF ESSENTIAL ITEMS

Even though the emphasis is on packing light, there are things which have to be carried for any trip. Here is our list of essentials:

• Passport/Visa or any other ID

• Any other paper work that might be required on a trip like permits, hotel reservation confirmations etc.

• Medicines – all your prescription medicines and emergency kit, especially if you are travelling with children

• Medical or vaccination records

• Money in foreign currency if travelling to a different country

• Tickets- Email or Message them to your phone

50. MAKE THE MOST OF YOUR TRIP

Wherever you are going, whatever you hope to do we encourage you to embrace it whole-heartedly. Take in the scenery, the culture and above all, enjoy your time away from home.

On a long journey even a straw weighs heavy.

-Spanish Proverb

PACKING AND PLANNING TIPS

A Week before Leaving

- Arrange for someone to take care of pets and water plants

- Stop mail and newspaper

- Notify Credit Card companies where you are going.

- Change your thermostat settings

- Car inspected, oil is changed, and tires have the correct pressure.

- Passports and id is up to date.

- Pay bills.

- Copy important items and download travel Apps.

- Start collecting small bills for tips

Right Before Leaving

- Clean out refrigerator.

- Empty garbage cans.

- Lock windows.

- Make sure you have the right ID with you.

- Bring cash for tips.

- Remember travel documents.

- Lock door behind you.

- Remember wallet.

- Unplug items in house and pack chargers.

>TOURIST

READ OTHER
GREATER THAN A TOURIST
BOOKS

Greater Than a Tourist San Miguel de Allende Guanajuato Mexico:
50 Travel Tips from a Local by Tom Peterson

Greater Than a Tourist – Lake George Area New York USA:
50 Travel Tips from a Local by Janine Hirschklau

Greater Than a Tourist – Monterey California United States:
50 Travel Tips from a Local by Katie Begley

Greater Than a Tourist – Chanai Crete Greece:
50 Travel Tips from a Local by Dimitra Papagrigoraki

Greater Than a Tourist – The Garden Route Western Cape Province
South Africa:
50 Travel Tips from a Local by Li-Anne McGregor van Aardt

Greater Than a Tourist – Sevilla Andalusia Spain:
50 Travel Tips from a Local by Gabi Gazon

Greater Than a Tourist – Kota Bharu Kelantan Malaysia:
50 Travel Tips from a Local by Aditi Shukla

Children's Book: Charlie the Cavalier Travels the World by Lisa
Rusczyk

>TOURIST

> TOURIST

Visit Greater Than a Tourist for Free Travel Tips
http://GreaterThanATourist.com

Sign up for the Greater Than a Tourist Newsletter for discount days, new books, and travel information:
http://eepurl.com/cxspyf

Follow us on Facebook for tips, images, and ideas:
https://www.facebook.com/GreaterThanATourist

Follow us on Pinterest for travel tips and ideas:
http://pinterest.com/GreaterThanATourist

Follow us on Instagram for beautiful travel images:
http://Instagram.com/GreaterThanATourist

>TOURIST

> TOURIST

Please leave your honest review of this book on Amazon and Goodreads. Please send your feedback to GreaterThanaTourist@gmail.com as we continue to improve the series. Thank you. We appreciate your positive and constructive feedback. Thank you.

METRIC CONVERSIONS

TEMPERATURE

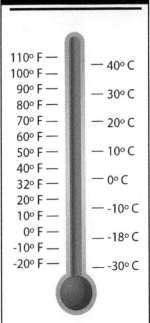

110° F — — 40° C
100° F —
90° F — — 30° C
80° F —
70° F — — 20° C
60° F —
50° F — — 10° C
40° F —
32° F — — 0° C
20° F —
10° F — — -10° C
0° F —
-10° F — — -18° C
-20° F — — -30° C

To convert F to C:

Subtract 32, and then multiply by 5/9 or .5555.

To Convert C to F:

Multiply by 1.8 and then add 32.

32F = 0C

LIQUID VOLUME

To Convert:..................Multiply by
U.S. Gallons to Liters................ 3.8
U.S. Liters to Gallons 26
Imperial Gallons to U.S. Gallons 1.2
Imperial Gallons to Liters....... 4.55
Liters to Imperial Gallons 22
1 Liter = .26 U.S. Gallon
1 U.S. Gallon = 3.8 Liters

DISTANCE

To convert ....Multiply by
Inches to Centimeters 2.54
Centimeters to Inches 39
Feet to Meters....................... .3
Meters to Feet 3.28
Yards to Meters 91
Meters to Yards 1.09
Miles to Kilometers 1.61
Kilometers to Miles............ .62
1 Mile = 1.6 km
1 km = .62 Miles

WEIGHT

1 Ounce = .28 Grams
1 Pound = .4555 Kilograms
1 Gram = .04 Ounce
1 Kilogram = 2.2 Pounds

TRAVEL QUESTIONS

- Do you bring presents home to family or friends after a vacation?

- Do you get motion sick?

- Do you have a favorite billboard?

- Do you know what to do if there is a flat tire?

- Do you like a sun roof open?

- Do you like to eat in the car?

- Do you like to wear sun glasses in the car?

- Do you like toppings on your ice cream?

- Do you use public bathrooms?

- Did you bring your cell phone and does it have power?

- Do you have a form of identification with you?

- Have you ever been pulled over by a cop?

- Have you ever given money to a stranger on a road trip?

- Have you ever taken a road trip with animals?

- Have you ever went on a vacation alone?

- Have you ever run out of gas?

- If you could move to any place in the world, where would it be?

- If you could travel anywhere in the world, where would you travel?

- If you could travel in any vehicle, which one would it be?

- If you had three things to wish for from a magic genie, what would they be?

- If you have a driver's license, how many times did it take you to pass the test?

- What are you the most afraid of on vacation?

- What do you want to get away from the most when you are on vacation?

- What foods smells bad to you?

- What item to you bring on ever trip with you away from home?

- What makes you sleepy?

- What song would you love to hear on the radio when you're cruising on the highway?

- What travel job would you want the least?

- What will you miss most while you are away from home?

- What is something you always wanted to try?

- What is the best road side attraction that you ever saw?

- What is the farthest distance you ever biked?

- What is the farthest distance you ever walked?

- What is the weirdest thing you needed to buy while on vacation?

- What is your favorite candy?

- What is your favorite color car?

- What is your favorite family vacation?

- What is your favorite food in the world?

- What is your favorite gas station drink or food?

- What is your favorite license plate design?

- What is your favorite restaurant in the world?

- What is your favorite smell?

- What is your favorite song?

- What is your favorite sound that nature makes?

- What is your favorite thing to bring home from a vacation?

- What is your favorite vacation with friends?

- What is your favorite way to relax?

- What is your favorite weather conditions while driving?

- Where in the world would you rather never get to travel?

- Where is the farthest place you ever traveled in a car?

- Where is the farthest place you ever went North, South, East and West?

- Where is your favorite place in the world?

- Who is your favorite singer?

- Who taught you how to drive?

- Who will you miss the most while you are away?

- Who if the first person you will call when you get to your destination?

- Who brought you on your first vacation?

- Who likes to travel the most in your life?

- Would you rather be hot or cold?

- Would you rather drive above, below, or at the speed limited?

- Would you rather drive on a highway or a back road?

- Would you rather go on a train or a boat?

- Would you rather go to the beach or the woods?

TRAVEL BUCKET LIST

1.

2.

3.

4.

5.

6.

7.

8.

9.

10.

NOTES